YOU'D *never* BELIEVE IT BUT...

there's a great bear in the sky

and other facts about stars

Designed and produced by
Aladdin Books Ltd
28 Percy Street
London W1P 0LD

*First published in the United States
in 1998 by*
Copper Beech Books,
an imprint of
The Millbrook Press
2 Old New Milford Road
Brookfield, Connecticut 06804

Designed by
David West Children's Book Design
Computer illustrations
Stephen Sweet (Simon Girling & Associates)
Picture Research
Brooks Krikler Research
Project Editor
Sally Hewitt
Editor
Jon Richards

Printed in Belgium

Library of Congress Cataloging-in-Publication Data
Taylor, Helen, 1932-
There is a great bear in th sky and other facts about
stars / by Helen Taylor ; illustrated by Stephen Sweet.
p. cm. — (You'd never believe it but—)
Includes index.
Summary: An introduction to astronomy, with information
about such topics as how stars are born and how they die, why
stars twinkle, and how to identify constellations.
ISBN 0-7613-0863-6 (lib. bdg.)
1. Astronomy—Juvenile literature. 2. Stars—Juvenile literature.
3. Constellations—Juvenile literature.
[1. Astronomy. 2. Stars. 3. Constellations.]
I. Sweet, Stephen, 1965- ill. II. Title. III. Series.
QB46.T395 1998   98-27548
523.8—dc21   CIP AC
5 4 3 2 1

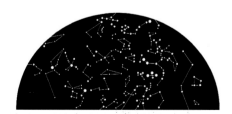

YOU'D *never* BELIEVE IT BUT...

there's a great bear in the sky

and other facts about stars

Helen Taylor

COPPER BEECH BOOKS
BROOKFIELD, CONNECTICUT

Contents

Introduction

Look into the night sky and you will see hundreds

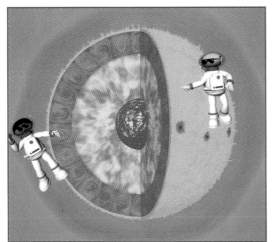

and hundreds of tiny points of light. Most of these are stars. If it's dark and clear enough, you might also be able to see a milky band stretching across the night sky. This is formed from billions and billions of stars too distant to see separately.

Join Jack and Jo as they discover some fantastic facts about stars.

FUN PROJECTS
Wherever you see this sign, it means there is a fun project that you can do. Each project will help you to understand more about the subject.
WARNING:
Never look directly at the sun. Its powerful light will damage your eyes!

Looking at the sky

While the night sky is filled with stars, these same stars seem to disappear in the daytime. They are still there, but their light is too faint to see in the bright light from our nearest star, the sun.

The stars are twinkling.

Stars seem to twinkle because their light has to shine through the air. If you were to stand on the moon, you could see the stars shining steadily. This is because there is no atmosphere to make them twinkle.

Sometimes, you can see the moon during the day. This is because it reflects enough of the sun's light to make it bright enough to be visible in daylight.

You'd never believe it but...

Sunlight shining through the atmosphere makes the sky look blue. This is because the tiny particles that make up air scatter the color blue in sunlight.

> I can't see the stars in the daytime.

 NIGHT AND DAY

1. Imagine the light from a flashlight is a star. Shine it in bright daylight. You can't see its light very clearly.

2. Now shine the flashlight at night or with the drapes closed. The flashlight will shine very brightly now.

What is a star?

A star is a huge ball of burning gas. Our star, the sun, has many objects, including planets, which orbit around it. They make up the solar system. Some of these objects appear to shine, but they are not stars.

Shooting stars aren't really stars. They're tiny pieces of rock from space that bump into the atmosphere and burn up, leaving a fiery streak.

The earth and the moon are shining!

At certain times of the year, you can see the planets Mars and Venus.

No, they're not. They're reflecting the light from the sun.

You'd never believe it but...

Stars shine with different colored lights, and some shine more brightly than others. Blue stars are very hot, while red stars are cooler.

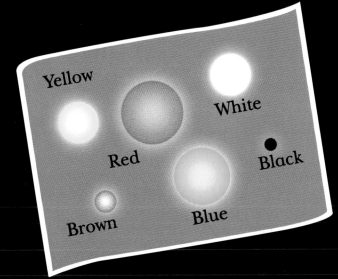

Yellow

White

Red

Black

Brown

Blue

SHINING PLANETS

1. Hang a ball from the ceiling in a darkened room.
2. Now shine a flashlight onto it. When the flashlight is turned on, you will be able to see the ball because it is reflecting the flashlight's light. The same thing happens when a planet or a moon reflects the sun's light.

Seeing stars

You can look at the stars through binoculars or telescopes. They make faraway objects look closer and clearer. Astronomers use more powerful equipment to look into space. They can see far more than you can.

Many large telescopes are built on the tops of very high mountains. Up here the air is very thin, and astronomers can get a clearer picture of the stars.

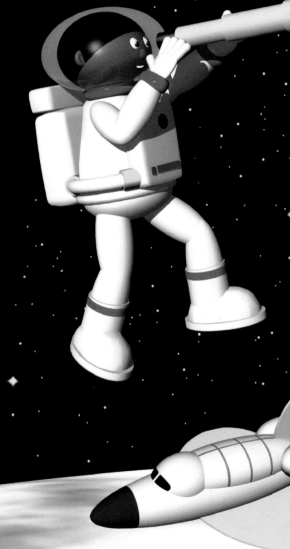

You can see a lot more stars up here.

You'd never believe it but...

There's a telescope in space. The Hubble Space Telescope orbits the earth high above the atmosphere.

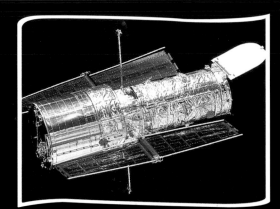

There's no atmosphere to make them look fuzzy.

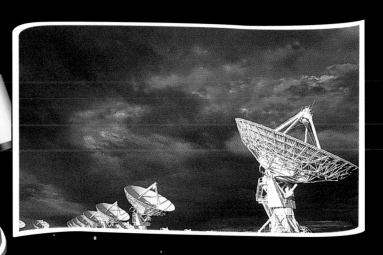

Huge metal dishes called radio telescopes can detect invisible objects.

BIGGER THINGS

You can understand how a telescope works by using a magnifying glass. Hold it over some items and see what it does to them. The glass lens in the magnifying glass bends light and makes the items look bigger. A telescope has several lenses to make the objects appear even larger.

Constellations

When you look up at the night sky, you might be able to see the stars arranged in patterns. These patterns are called constellations. Even though the stars appear to be close together, they are actually unbelievably huge distances apart.

I can see a big bear and a little bear.

You'd never believe it but...

There's a great bear in the sky. The star patterns are named after characters in ancient Greek stories. You can see them on a star map.

A planetarium is a huge room where people can go to see the night sky at any time of the day. Pictures of the stars are projected onto the ceiling.

I can see Perseus.

You'd never believe it but...

Long ago, people believed that night was caused by a giant curtain being drawn across the sky. They thought that the stars were holes in this curtain.

Astronomers can take special photos that show that the stars seem to move in circles. However, these circles are caused by the spinning of the earth.

Spinning in space

Everything in space spins. The earth spins around every 24 hours. It also spins around the sun in a path called an orbit. The earth, as well as the other eight planets that make up the solar system, is kept spinning in its orbit by a force called gravity.

WATCHING THE EARTH SPIN

Stick a piece of tracing paper against a window and draw the outline of the horizon. Mark the position of a star on it. One hour later, mark the position of the star again. You will see that the star appears to have moved.

I hope the ball doesn't fall off.

The string keeps the ball going around, just like a planet going around the sun.

Our solar system

Pluto

Neptune

Mercury

Sun

Earth

Saturn

Mars

Venus

Jupiter

Uranus

Woof!

There are nine planets that go around the sun. There is also a band of small rocky asteroids called the Asteroid Belt.

You'd never believe it but...

Rockets need to go very quickly to leave the earth. To reach orbit, or even beyond, a spaceship needs the blast of powerful rocket motors to push it fast enough to escape the pull of the earth. Otherwise, it would fall back down.

Our nearest star

The sun is actually our nearest star, even though it looks very different from the nighttime stars. It gives us all our heat and light.

The sun only seems bigger than the other stars because it is much nearer to us than they are.

JUST HOW BIG?

The earth is much smaller than the sun. To give you an idea of its size, if the sun were the size of a soccer ball, then the earth would only be the size of a pea. The distance between the sun and the earth would then be about one-third as long as a soccer field.

Sun

Earth

Why is the sun so big in the sky?

The stars that appear in the night sky look like tiny points of light. In fact, they are huge objects, many of them bigger than the sun.

Because it's so close to us.

SIZE AND DISTANCE
Distance can make objects appear bigger or smaller. Ask a friend to stand close to you. Now compare them to a far-off tree — he or she may look as big as the tree. Now get them to stand next to the tree — he or she now seems to be smaller than the tree.

You'd never believe it but...
Light from the sun takes eight minutes to reach us. However, it takes light from the next nearest star over four years to reach us.

Inside the sun

Surface

The sun is really a huge ball of burning gas. The gas starts to burn in the middle of the sun, the core. The heat then travels to the outside of the sun before being given off into space, giving us heat and light.

Core

Phew! I'm getting very hot!

WARNING
Always put on some sunblock when you go out on a hot sunny day.

The sun sends out rays that can harm us. The earth's atmosphere acts like a shield and protects us from many of these rays.

Yes, if a spaceship tried to land on the sun, it would melt quickly!

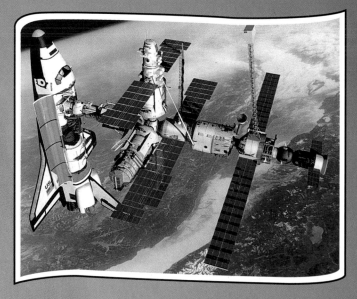

Spaceships can use the sun to make power. Special solar panels can change sunlight into electricity that can be used to power a spaceship in space.

Sometimes, spots can appear on the sun. These sunspots are where the surface is slightly cooler and therefore darker.

You'd never believe it but...

The sun keeps us alive. Every living thing on the earth depends on the sun to supply it with heat, light and energy. Without the sun, everything would die!

A star is born

There are enormous clouds of gas and dust in space, called nebulae, where stars are born. Dust and gas are pulled together into spinning blobs by a force called gravity. The blobs become hotter and hotter. After millions of years, they become hot enough to give out light and heat, and a star is born.

Was the sun born like this?

The Great Nebula, which can be seen in the costellation Orion, is a huge cloud of gas and dust where stars are being formed. This star nursery glows brightly with the light of newborn stars. Over a very long time, these stars will grow old and die.

The Great Nebula in Orion

Yes. It took around 5 billion years to get to this stage.

You'd never believe it but...

There's a horse's head in space. The Horsehead Nebula is a dark cloud that blocks out light from the stars behind it. It can be found in the constellation called Orion.

Death of a star

A star usually dies with a bang. The bigger the star, the bigger the bang. Before it dies, a star will swell up, changing color to orange and then red before it explodes.

Just before a star explodes, it swells into a red giant star.

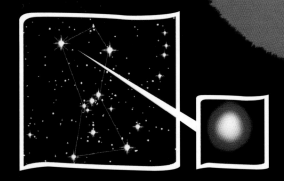

You'd never believe it but...

There are red giants in space. A red giant star called Betelgeuse in the constellation of Orion is 500 times as wide as our own sun!

How long before the sun dies?

Oh, it will last for at least another 4 billion years!

A star explosion is called a nova. If a really big star explodes, it is called a supernova. Supernovae can leave black holes behind them.

Novae leave behind white dwarf stars that cool and fade away.

Novae and supernovae throw off clouds of debris when they explode. This debris forms patterns around the cooling remains of the dying star.

Strange stars

There are some strange stars in space. Some send out flashes of radiation. Others are the remains of powerful star explosions. A black hole is the remains of a star. It has such a strong force of gravity that nothing can escape its pull — not even light!

Don't go too close — you might get sucked in.

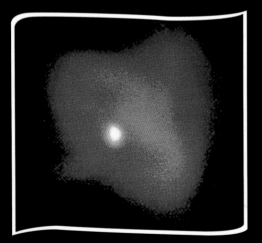

Pulsars are strange stars that are like lighthouses in space. They spin quickly, sending out powerful beams of radiation.

I know. Even light can't escape from its pull.

You'd never believe it but...

When astronomers first detected the radiation from pulsars, they thought that they were messages from aliens in outer space!

WHAT IS GRAVITY?

Throw a ball into the air and the earth's gravity will pull it down. Gravity is the force that attracts objects to each other.

The Milky Way

The sun and all the stars that we can see at night belong to a group of billions of stars called a galaxy. We call the galaxy that we belong to the Milky Way. It is shaped like a spiral, and we live in one of its spiral arms.

There are a lot of galaxies in space. They can be shaped like a spiral or a blob called an ellipse.

On a clear, moonless night, you can see a misty band across the sky. This is our edge-on view of the billions of stars that make up the Milky Way.

How many stars are in the Milky Way?

There are about 100 to 200 billion of them.

Sun

You'd never believe it but...
It takes light from our nearest galaxy over 2 million years to reach us. Our neighboring galaxy is called the Andromeda Galaxy.

MAKING A SPIRAL GALAXY
Cut a notch out of a circle of cardboard and stick the two ends together to form a cone. Now place the cone on a pencil stuck to some paper.

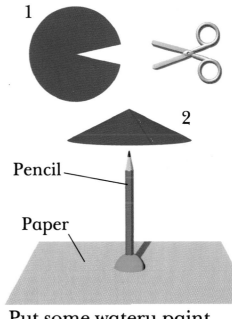

1

2

Pencil

Paper

Put some watery paint on the cone and spin the cone. Watch the paint form a spiral.

Using stars

When you get to know the stars well enough, you can use them to find your way around the night sky. People have also used the stars to find their way around on the ground.

Sailors and explorers have used the stars to find their way for a long time. Using an object called an astrolabe, they could figure out where they were.

Look! There's the North Star.

You'd never believe it but...

People in different hemispheres see different stars. People in the northern hemisphere cannot see the Southern Cross.

Home must be over there to the west.

HOW TO FIND THE NORTH STAR
In the northern hemispere, find the constellation called the Great Bear. Part of the Great Bear, called the Big Dipper or the Plow, points to the North Star. This star sits directly above the north pole. So when you see it, you can find which way is north.

North
Star

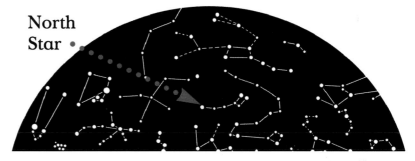

FINDING THE SOUTH POLE
In the southern hemispere, find the constellation called the Southern Cross. Two of this constellation's stars point to a part of the sky that lies over the south pole. So wherever you see the Southern Cross, you can find out which way is south.

Southern
Cross

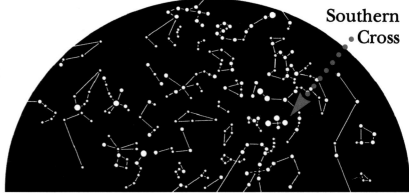

Glossary

Atmosphere

The atmosphere is a layer of air that is wrapped around the earth. It is essential for life on Earth. It keeps the earth warm and protects us from the sun's harmful rays.

Black holes

A black hole forms when a giant star collapses into a tiny space. A black hole has such a strong pull of gravity that it sucks everything in, even light.

Constellation

A constellation is a group of stars that look as if they are arranged together in a pattern, when we look at them from the earth. Long ago, the Greeks named the constellations after characters from their stories.

Galaxy

A galaxy is a group of stars. The sun belongs to a galaxy called the Milky Way. The Milky Way is just one of billions of galaxies in the universe.

Gravity

Gravity is a force that attracts objects toward each other. The earth's gravity pulls everything down toward its center. The earth moves around the sun because the sun's gravity is pulling the earth toward it.

Moon

The moon is the nearest object in space to the earth. The earth's gravity pulls the moon, making it circle around the earth.

Nebula

Nebulae are enormous clouds of dust and gas in space. New stars are born from spinning dust and gas inside these clouds.

Nova

A nova is a star that suddenly becomes very bright. It shines brilliantly for a while before it fades away and dies.

Planet

A planet is a huge ball of rock, metal, or gas in space. A planet has no heat and light of its own. The earth is one of nine planets that move around the sun.

Shooting star

A shooting star is not really a star at all. It is a piece of space dust called a meteor that flares up suddenly as it falls through Earth's atmosphere.

Solar system

The solar system is the sun and the nine planets that move around it. The sun's powerful gravity pulls all the planets toward it and stops them from floating off into space.

Solar panel

Solar panels turn energy from sunlight into electricity.

Star

A star is a massive ball of burning gas. There are billions of stars in space. They come in different sizes and colors.

Telescope

A telescope makes objects look larger and clearer. The Hubble Space Telescope is a large telescope in space that sends pictures of the universe back to Earth.

Index

PHOTO CREDITS:

Abbreviations: t-top, m-middle, b-bottom, r-right, l-left, c-center

7 all, 12, 14, 19b, 25 – Roger Vlitos. 8, 17 – Pictor International. 10, 11m, 18 – Frank Spooner. 11t, 15, 19t, 22, 23 – NASA. 13t, 24, 26, 27, 28b – Science Photo Library. 13m, 28t – Mary Evans Picture Library.